Ashes to Beauty

Lora Brand

©Lora Brand [2010] by Lora Brand

All rights reserved

No portion of this book may be reproduced, distributed or transmitted, in any form or by any means, including photocopying, recording or other electronic methods, without written permission from the publisher or author, except in the case of brief quotations and certain other non- commercial uses permitted by copyright law.

The advice and strategies contained in this publication may not be suitable for your situation. You should consult with a professional when appropriate, Neither the publisher nor the author shall be liable for any loss or profit or any other commercial damages, including but not limited to special, incidental, consequential, personal, or other damages.

Title   Ashes to Beauty

ISBN: 978-1-7637864-1-7

Book Cover by [Lora Brand]

Illustrations by [Lora Brand]

[2] Edition [lora Brand]

Poetry (Lora Brand 2025)

Christian life Anecdotes

Contents

Author's note 3
Acknowledgements 5
Introduction 7
Foundations 11
    Bible Verse - Luke 6:47-49 (New King James Version) 14
The Fire Pit 15
Ashes Poem 16
Ashes to Beauty 17
    Bible Verse - Psalm 34:6 (New International Version) 18
Ashes of Hate 21
    Hatred Poem 25
Ashes of Loneliness/Isolation 27
    Loneliness' Poem 29
    Bible Verse Psalm 23 (New International Version) 30
Ashes of Rejection 31
    Destiny poem 33
    Rejection Poem 35
Ashes of Regret 36
    Regret Poem 39
Ashes of Grief 40
    Grief Poem 43

Ashes of Shame 45
    Shame Poem..47
Bible Verse- Psalm 91:1 (New International Version).........49
    Peace Poem..50

Author's note

This book is written in the hope that the reader can identify the destructive nature of many emotions that we sometimes have to face. The poetry captures the rawness of a wounded heart, then leading the heart to a place of hope.

Once identified, then hopefully have the courage to face these emotions, and seek help from sources that best suit individual needs.

Circumstances of life may cause us to feel and experience the torment of emotional turmoil. It simply means that you and I are human.

For those of you who read this book and have, or had faith in Christ Jesus, and are walking through the valley of ashes, I encourage you to continue to seek after the ways of God.

To continue to allow His love and His grace walk you through.

For those of you who read this and have not experienced Faith and hope in Jesus Christ, I encourage you that whatever valleys of life you face, there is always hope.

I pray that you will find good counsel and friends that will walk with you and encourage you, as you face life's ashes.

Acknowledgements

Many thanks to my family, from whom I have learned much. To my husband who, through conflicts of life and marriage I have gained confidence and strength. To Lisa, my friend who has always challenged me with my thoughts and attitudes.

Especially to my three grown-up children, who have always been my inspiration to strive to be the best I could possibly be.

I have learned and gained much from you, Dale, Adam and Sarah. It is my honor and pride to be your mother.

Many thanks to my friends who have always been there and walked with me out of and through the ashes.

The one I thank the most is my Lord, my Redeemer who has been the closest to my heart, who knows all.

Introduction

I have lived and breathed the very essence of the contents of this book. It is written not out of study or education but out of life itself.

For most of my life I have built a foundation of faith, hope and love in Jesus Christ. As a young child I learned about God and yet did not really know him. In a childlike manner I trusted in His protection and peace, and yes, I would feel peace when all around me was turmoil and trouble.

Then I grew older, and life was before me. Thinking I knew it all, I married at 16, only to find that marriage and children could not fill all the gaps and voids hidden in one's heart.

Years passed on with many trying times, as well as the loss of a beautiful sister whose life ended at 39. I learned what it is to walk through the many ashes which I now write about.

I learned to put my trust in the promises of God's word according to scripture.

In saying this I had to consciously make a choice to believe the truth of God's word. I had to remind myself to focus on the Word of God, rather than the circumstances around.

I learned that if I was to put my trust in God, that my actions and words would also need to line up with God's word, to the best of my ability.

This did not come easy, and many times I would feel disheartened, disappointed, and disillusioned as time did not move quickly enough.

I understood though, that I by myself could not walk through these valleys that I call ashes. I recognized that I needed the help of God who loves me and all humanity.

I knew that not only does God provide a way to navigate life successfully through the bible, but also, He promises to send a comforter/ a helper. This is the Holy Spirit.

It was through the Holy Spirit that I would feel and know strength, love, hope and assurance, and that in due time these ashes will pass.

These ashes did pass, and while walking through them it was not always the way I would have thought or planned.

I thank my God and the Lord Jesus Christ for without him I dare not hope.

If you have hope, even the tiniest seed of hope, you can continue.

For my people perish for lack of knowledge. (Proverbs 29:18)

It was this hope and faith of the promise, that God will work together for good, all things for those who love him and live according to his will and purpose. (Romans 8:28), that has carried me through the years. My life has been built on the foundations of Christ Jesus and His word and promises, and through His Holy Spirit enabling me to be restored from ashes to beauty.

Foundations

A fire rages quickly, consuming what was once a beautiful home set on a hill in a quiet, peaceful suburb.

Noisily disturbing neighboring homes, as many come and watch in horror. Loud explosions pollute the air as windows blow out from their very frames. The stench of thick smoke billowing like chimneys.

At last, the firefighters arrive, hoping to quench the appetite of this raging fire. Hoses spraying from several angles, dumping gallons of water into the very mouth of this raging tyrant. Finally, what seemed like hours were beginning to pay off. All that remains now is small red smoldering embers. One by one, diminishing as water continues to rain on their very core.

"Now what shall remain?" Onlookers whisper and talk, hoping to hear the outcome this disaster leaves.

Months later all that is now seen is the desolation of this once splendid home.

Burnt out weak structures stand with piles of ash on a foundation that is solid and unshakable. Where there were once lush leaves and beautiful gardens surrounding this home, now grows thorns and thistles, overgrown grass and unkempt shrubs.

The decay is quickly seen by those who once stopped and admire all the beauty this property holds. Now they simply drive past helpless and powerless to assist in any restoration of this once splendid property.

Will a restoration take place, or will it remain as prey for feral animals to take refuge in? Will it remain unkempt until it looks as though there never was anything of value ever there?

The foundation remains strong and so it is the decision of the Landlord, whether he will have the courage to start over and rebuild again.

****

Our lives are very much like this home as disaster comes and shakes our very being.

Sometimes to the point of leaving empty piles of ashes.

Friends may surround us but are helpless in restoring our life. Not helpless because they do not care, but simply they do not have the means to do so. They love but cannot carry the ashes that we bear. Through no fault of theirs they look on and life continues; unknown to them is the depth and reality that those ashes have brought.

Like in that desolate land, isolation sets in, leaving one standing alone even though you are not. A foundation remains of your core beliefs and ideals. Will that foundation allow you to rebuild your life, or will it let you down, leaving you lifeless and unable to restore.

Bible Verse - Luke 6:47-49 (New King James Version)

"Whoever comes to me, and hears my sayings and does them, I will show you whom he is like. He is like a man building a house, who dug deep and laid the foundation on the rock. And when the flood arose, the stream beat vehemently against that house, and could not shake it, for it was founded on the rock. But he who heard and did nothing is like a man who built a house on the earth without a foundation, against which the stream beat vehemently; And immediately it fell, and the ruin of that house was great."

The Fire Pit

A fire pit has many uses but once it has burned out all the wood it remains a pile of coal and ashes.

These ashes, left unattended, will eventually contaminate and spoil any ability to be useful.

No longer can these ashes be used for good fertilizer, for soap and cleaning products.

The elements of the weather, sand, rain, wind and dirt have spoiled their very purpose.

These ashes are now left to be scattered, thrown out or simply lie dormant, with no new growth springing forth out of them

Ashes Poem

The taste of ashes bitter and bare
From grief and loss, who really does care?
Ashes of regret from the choices we made
Consequences and pain from the foundation we laid

Ashes of hope and dreams destroyed
Leaving your soul empty and void
Ashes of disappointment and failure to carry
Day by day seeming to tarry

Ashes of betrayal and a broken trust
Is there anyone fair and truly just?
Ashes of a life wounded and marred
Leaving one's emotions crippled and scarred

Ashes of loneliness as isolation sets in
Does this end or can I begin?
Begin to dream new hopes and dreams
Not glancing back at what it seems

Out of ashes to rise and look ahead
As new growth sprouts from what once was dead
A promise of hope from the Father above
Under His shadow, covered with love

Beauty for ashes, the oil of joy as well
Poured out on you as a sweet fragrant smell
Come to Him with your ashes of dust
Giving them up is really a must

For dormant they lie contaminating much
Spoiling your life and all that you touch.

Ashes to Beauty

> "I will put beautiful crowns on their heads in place of ashes. I will anoint them with oil to give them gladness instead of sorrow. I will give them a spirit of praise instead of a spirit of sadness. They will be like oak trees that are strong and straight."
>
> Isaiah 61:3

****

A crown is a reward or prize, a token of public honor. Some passages refer to it as an emblem of life, joy, reward and glory (Vine's Concise Dictionary).

Whether you believe in God or whether you do not, life happens. Good and bad comes to all of us.

It is a myth to think that just because we believe in Jesus Christ, and that we are followers of Him, that we will automatically be exempt from life's troubles.

Bible Verse -Psalm 34:6 (New International Version)

"A righteous man may have many troubles, but the Lord delivers him from them all". Psalm 34:6

Jesus said, "I have come that you may have life and life abundantly". John 10:10

This verse also tells us about the thief coming to rob, steal and destroy, as opposing to Jesus coming to give life in a full measure.

This does not mean we will have everything we want, but we can successfully walk through every valley that we face.

Abundance is a state of being of your heart and soul.

****

"Life has dished out many an uncertain time, and I have learned to walk in this abundance over the years, where the enemy tried to steal my joy, peace, sanity and well-being, Jesus came and through His word, His truth, and His Spirit gave me abundance."

"I can truly say I can feel the crown that He has bestowed on me." Not because I am different to anyone else, but because I believe time is the very essence of bringing one to a place of peace.

Everyone is different and I believe there is no formula except to continue to read, obey and trust God's word to the best of your ability and understanding.

****

I have never met anyone who has not experienced some form of grief, disappointment, loss, sorrow, rejection or pain.

Whatever circumstances we may find ourselves in, we can grow successfully through those storms.

When faced with trials we must make choices.

Trials bring out many emotions within us, which often can be like a small seed that

takes root within your very soul. Emotions are good if released in a positive way.
If released negatively, they can be dangerous to yourself and to others.

There is a way to navigate through those emotions that will cause you much joy and peace.

This is the way designed by God.

To put trust in Him and hand over your ashes for His beauty, your mourning for His oil of joy, your spirit of heaviness, for His garment of praise.

This takes faith and courage to trust someone enough to share the secrets of your heart

This may also come at a personal cost, as it is often easier to ignore the issues faced or find a quick-fixed solution.

God's word never lies and has an answer to help us through every trial we face.

I have found that it is never easy to walk the right road, and as tiring and useless as it may sometimes seem, it is the most rewarding.

Ashes of Hate

Hatred simply is not just a word; it is a very real destructive emotion.

It means to "set against" something or someone. The strong sense of the word typifies the emotion of intense jealousy, or bitter disdain, which could plot murder or torture (Vine's Concise Dictionary.

Hatred is not something that you deliberately set out to plan. Hatred is an emotion that has taken root, and sprouted from a seed, e.g. jealousy, betrayal, abuse. Hatred springs forth out of the ashes of these seeds hidden deep within the heart.

Like that fire pit, these ashes if left dormant and unattended contaminate and wreak havoc on your soul.

Forgiveness is the key to bringing forth new growth out of these ashes. Forgiving someone is a choice that is often very difficult to make. This may seem impossible or unjust, and I would encourage anyone struggling with the concept of this, to seek advice from a pastor, church leader or read books on forgiveness.

I have found that once I had made that choice to forgive, I had to constantly re-align my thoughts with God's word. I had to choose to speak and act according to forgiveness, going against the thoughts that could easily lure me in the opposite direction. Time soon passed and those thoughts faded away as though they had never existed.

Hatred is a dangerous place to sit in. It can cause a brother to murder a brother as in the bible story of Cain and Able. Through the seed of jealousy, leading to hate, this event took place.

Hatred can lead us into destructive lifestyles, crime, drugs, alcoholism etc.

Lifestyles that diminish who we really are and spoil our ability to be all that we had once hoped and dreamed of.

Hatred can replace the foundation that was once strong into one that crumbles under its demands.

Hatred does nothing for the one who may have caused this seed to spring forth but does everything to keep you bound and destroy your very existence.

Hatred is like the flame engulfing that once splendid home and turning it into a pile of ash, reducing it to nothing. It is the decision of the owner of this home whether to restore it or not.

It lies with you to decide as to the restoration of your soul. Do we ignore the problem, bury our head in the sand or do we face the very issue that lies before us?

****

If your foundation is sandy with nothing to hope in or hold on to, then I encourage you to begin to build a new foundation that is full of hope and love.

If your foundation has begun on the hope and promise of Jesus Christ, then I encourage you to continue and allow that foundation to become even stronger.
Dare to trust and allow Him to rebuild from those ashes of hate.
Even the strongest foundations under cyclonic and adverse weather conditions are shaken up.

The Lord promises that even a heart full of hatred can be turned around. "I will give you a heart of flesh instead of a heart of stone". (Ezekiel 11:19. NKJ)

All He asks is for us to surrender that heart to him and He is faithful to do the rest. Nothing is impossible. Even the hardest of hearts can become soft again.

Hatred Poem

Hate is a poison eating away at your core
Devouring all that's good, hungering for more
Hate buries deep in the depth of your soul
Destroying your ability to be rational and whole

Where does this come from? This hatred in one's heart
As a seedling it grows from the very start
Watered and nourished from thoughts deep within
Playing the same song over and over again

Behind the mask of hatred are the choices we make
Lifestyles of living reflect the risks that we take
Steering our path as a bridle on a horse
Taking control of our will by force

You hurt me bad, for this I will never forgive
Lost in memories and thoughts each day that I live
Entangled in a web of a plan to be free
With the light growing dim, I now barely see

How can I hide from this hatred so deep?
A bourbon, a whiskey my mind now sleeps
Then I awake, alas before my very eyes
Only to find that this was all lies

A lie from your enemy, who is the author of hate
Luring you in at a very fast rate
His aim is to destroy who you really are
Opposing the one who brought you this far

This one is the deliverer of your very soul
Taking back all the enemy stole
A way through the sludge, the torment the hate
Encouraging you, that it is never too late

Amongst all the anguish, the pain and the sorrow
There is a way for you to follow
Hand it over to the judge of all man
Yes, it is hard, but I know you can

Ashes of Loneliness/Isolation

There are times in our life when we may feel we are isolated and removed from everyone.

In a sense, we may be. What we experience and feel is so deep that it sets us apart from those around us

We cannot explain it in words, nor can we make circumstances disappear. We know that we must walk through these valleys, regardless of whatever it strips from our very core.

Even though we are not alone, it seems as though we are.

We need to find hope in that which is good. Find those friends that will stand with us.

They may not understand the valley or even know what we are experiencing, but they are there. They love us. Accept their love without expecting them to know or understand the depth of your valley.

The most relevant knowledge is to know that God stands with us. He is for us, not against us. Learn to tell him the secrets of our hearts, what we think, feel and believe.

Spill it all, for only then do we give Him permission to act on our behalf concerning these things.

We will not be disappointed, and we will begin a new journey of trust, as we surrender these things to Him.

Ecclesiastes Chapter 1 tells of life and its seasons. There is a time for everything: sadness, joy, grief, laughter and much more. The difference will be in the choice we make as to how we will walk through these seasons.

Loneliness' Poem

Friends' friends all around
Loneliness within not making a sound
Isolation, fears, who could possibly have known
The emotional turmoil not outwardly shown

Solitary confinement in the despair of one's heart
Not a whisper, not a word setting you apart
Company around but what could they know
Of a sorrow so deep with nowhere to go

A journey to walk through this valley of despair
Shattered hopes and dreams not always fair
Where do I go to find rest for my soul?
To fill this void and this gaping hole

Do I hide in this valley covered with shame?
Do I look around for someone to blame?
Do I end my life and finish it for good?
Do I dull my senses as often as I could?

None of the above will bring rest for my mind
For there is only one who is truly good and kind
Come and drink the water He will give
Quenching your thirst, giving you reason to live

Whisper to Him all that holds you bound
For in Him freedom shall be found
Await then for Him to calm your mind
Peace at last you will surely find

Listen in your heart to the instructions that come
Gentle direction from the father's son
A way through the rubble, the mud and the slush
"Til at last rest and a quiet hush

Bible Verse Psalm 23 (New International Version)

    The Lord is my Shepherd. He gives me everything I need.

    He lets me lie down in the fields of green grass.

He leads me beside quiet waters. He gives me new strength. He guides me in right paths for the honor of His name.

Even though I walk through the deepest valley, I will not be afraid. You are with me; your rod and your staff comfort me.

You prepare a feast for me right in front of my enemies. You pour oil on my head. My cup runs over.

I am sure that your goodness and love will follow me, all the days of my life. And I will live in the house of the Lord forever.

Ashes of Rejection

Rejection comes in many forms. There is rejection from birth, even in the mother's womb. Adoption also causes rejection.

We may experience rejection from a spouse or loved one, from a friend or family member.

Job losses, lack of promotion and recognition feed rejection.

Some of these rejection issues are minor and easily dealt with, whilst others go deep into the heart.

The rejection that begins from childhood is often rooted deep into the very core of the heart of a grown man or woman.

Like those ashes lying dormant from that fire pit, they begin to get contaminated. Rather than being useful, those ashes have sprouted forth seeds of fear, insecurity, unworthiness and a lack of courage to live life to its fullest measure.

Rejection continues to grow and choke out our ability to have self-worth.
The ability to believe in and love ourselves is smothered in smoldering ashes. Ashes are like rejection, in the manner that they are often too hot to touch.
Sensitivity breeds where there is a hidden heart of rejection.

'Whatever a man thinks and believes in the heart. So shall he be.' (Proverbs 23:7)

We live and breathe out of what we believe about ourselves in the heart.
Jesus experienced all forms of rejection and yet He rose above. The fact that He was born in a way that brought shame to Joseph and Mary. The fact that He was born in a stable/barn. The fact that His life was despised by many since birth.
Jesus identifies with us and the true nature of rejection. He made himself an example of freedom from the pain of rejection.

Destiny poem

There is no mistake in your very birth
The fact that you are here on this earth
Planted by Him was your very seed
Destiny and history are your birthright creed

Why was I planted in trouble deep
Was the creator awake or half asleep?
Don't be fooled by the surrounds from which you came
Nor go looking for someone to blame

Not all may have been just as it should
Sin and darkness breeding nothing good
How could one survive? I must confess
Surrounded by the smell of a stinking mess

Let the aroma bring forth life not death
New hope arising with every breath
Come to Him, all is not lost
Even if attached is personal cost

To surrender those things that have shaped your mind
New truth in Him may you surely find
Give up those thoughts that have hampered your years
Stunting your growth, engulfing you with fears

You are who you are, accept this fact
Designed with purpose and nothing lacked

Rejection Poem

Rejection denies the acceptance of one
Unworthiness carrying the weight of a ton
Striving to keep you separate from love
Keeping you in a self-protected glove

Rejection apologizes even when right
Fear governing, is your plight
A passive approach rejection will take
For fear of always making a mistake

Rejection tells lies to keep the peace
Hoping conflict will then cease
Causing one to often hide
A life of loneliness coincide

Rejection drives you to hate yourself
Thinking you will always be left on the shelf
Never good enough for anyone to care
A burden of which you falsely bare

Rejection is a lie opposing your core
Robbing your life and closing the door
A door of possibilities, hopes and dreams
A life worth living, not as it seems

Rejection has stolen the direction of your heart
Blinding the truth from the very start
Fashioned and framed with destiny in mind
The truth being you are one of a kind

Formed from the beginning from your birth
Even before you enter this earth
Chosen by grace to be who you are
Accepted and loved by Him thus far

Ashes of Regret

Regret has a sting that does not allow us to move on and see other possibilities. Regret keeps us in the past, locking us out of our future.

All of us make mistakes or choices that carry consequences. Sometimes the consequences are not necessarily bad, but difficult to live through. Life may often be better if we did not choose certain paths.

Whilst other consequences may have a more severe impact on our lives.
These often bring deep regret and sorrow.

To live out our consequences, rather than running or escaping, has more value than we could possibly imagine. Wisdom is often gained through that season of consequence.

Far greater to have learned wisdom from walking through the valley than to remain crippled as bad decisions often lead to more bad decisions.

Continuing to look at past failures will blind your ability to see your future.

You run the risk of becoming dormant like those ashes from that fire pit. Eventually you will be contaminated and no longer see yourself useful/worthy of anything.

We need to forgive ourselves and move on and allow that experience to shape our future for the best.

If it is good enough for God to forgive us, then we owe it to ourselves to forgive us too. Through accepting His forgiveness for our sin and mistakes, we make room allowing His Grace and mercy to lead us on the right paths.

Sometimes it is difficult to accept His forgiveness because we are so hard on ourselves. We stand in the place of the judge, holding ourselves accountable and punishing ourselves as guilty for ever.

Even in the courts of law we serve a sentence for a time until pardoned. The key word here being pardoned, which means to be no longer guilty or held accountable for certain actions.

****

For God so loved the world that He gave His only begotten son. John 3:16

God gave His only son up for us - surely, we can give our ashes of regret up to Him.

Regret Poem

The path that you take from a life of regret
Hoping to erase, hoping to forget
Will often determine what lies ahead
Living an existence of a future now dead

The sting of regret shapes all that you do
Blinding your heart, hoping for anything new
Costing you much for those decisions once made
Memories of hopes and dreams, now often fade

Imprisoned in the mind without a key
To unlock all that one hoped to be
Wrestling within, is there any way out?
That's just and fair, holding no doubt

Haunting your thoughts as your past closes the door
Unable to fly free, like that eagle does soar
Dare to face life, ploughing through the thick snow
Accepting the road on which your life must go

For consequences last, but for only a season
During this time, you must find a reason
To hold your head up and walk out of self-blame
That has kept you bound and imprisoned in shame

Endless possibilities will always appear
Walk right on through, dismissing the fear
Shake off the ashes, the dirt and the grime
Enter a new season, not wasting more time

As your life has years yet to unfold
New history to make, new stories untold
Get a new perspective on your life at hand
And give to Him the leading command

Ashes of Grief

Many of us have had to face the death of a loved one. Grief often changes the direction of one's path forever.

Grief must be processed over time. There is no quick fix or easy solution. It does not just go away.

Grief can be dangerous if left dormant and unattended. It is something that needs to be released, shared, faced and healed. Not that you will ever forget that loved one, but the sting and bite of grief fades until it no longer holds you captive.

One thing I had learned in dealing with grief was to accept what I could not change. When my beautiful sister's life was suddenly cut short, there were many unanswered questions that plagued my mind.

At a quiet place beside the ocean, these questions I eventually spoke before the Lord. Then after pausing a few moments, I left those questions there on that beach with Him.

Peace came and I knew that I would eventually pass through this valley.

Grief is like an open wound and no amount of covering up will heal it. It is seen, it is felt, and it hurts.

We cannot escape the process of grief. Some people will grieve longer than others. Grief is not limited to time.

The wounds of grief will eventually heal. It is the scars and ashes that are left behind that often cause issues.

Death has come knocking at your door, often it is the circumstances around that death that leaves the most ashes.

In the case of a murder, a suicide or an accident, there are many unanswered questions. They invoke feelings and emotions that go deep into our hearts.

Not only are we dealing with the loss of one, but also the possibility of hate, anger, blame, something you may have never dreamed of or imagined that you would ever feel.

In these cases, I would encourage you to seek help to process some of these thoughts.

There are grief counsellors, books, Pastor's, Chaplains and church leaders, who will be valuable in assisting.

Grief Poem

Death has come knocking at your door
Gripped with sorrow, cannot take any more
That one who was once close to your heart
Now to be forever apart

Anguish of soul has taken hold
A heart now torn where once was bold
How to continue in this depth of despair?
How could this be? It just isn't fair

Struck down with pain, frozen with fear
How to let go of one held so dear?
Day by day grief takes its toll
Stealing all joy once held in the soul

Darkness closes in, no light to be found.
No words to speak, just silence, no sound
Condolences come from friends near and far
As tears now bottled and stuffed in a jar

Braving a front to cope with it all
Faking a smile and standing tall
If I could just hide and pretend it's all gone
Deceiving the eyes, where the light once shone

There is one, though, from whom you cannot hide
The emotions and feelings deep inside
Open your heart and find that secret place
As healing comes from His amazing grace

Dare to tell the anguish, the hell
Whisper, cry or – if you must-yell
Release the grief to the Almighty Shaddai
As healing will come as time passes by

Ashes of Shame

Shame is a strategy, to stop someone from achieving all that life has to offer.

Shame comes in many forms and takes root in our lives in various ways.

Shame also comes from mistakes made and choices that have had detrimental consequences to our self or others.

Shame is not something that is easy to shake off. It has an origin of where it began in our life, and this needs to be addressed.

A true person's character is often hidden behind a mask of shame.

Shame works hand in hand with guilt, making us feel like we are always wrong. Often this causes us to take the blame even when right, causing us to be apologetic where unnecessary.

Shame is not fair, nor is it just and it affects a very large part of our life. Jesus promises to lift us out of shame into the arms of His love.

1 John: 18-19 (New Living Translation)

Such love has no fear because perfect love expels all fear. If we are afraid, it is for fear of judgement, and this shows that His love has not been perfected in us. We love each other as a result of His loving us first"

His love for us is perfect and He chose to first love us.

Shame Poem

Shame holds you captive, a prisoner at best
Making you its victim, a personal quest
Shame is a liar that feeds your mind
Isolating your heart, leaving you blind

The truth of your beauty you cannot see
No value at all you think you will be
No courage to stand and fight for what's good
To live life with freedom as you know you should

Shame keeps you quiet, losing your rights
In open discussions and even in fights
Shame declares: You are not worthy
Shouting at you: You will never be free

To sing and to dance and be all who God made
Keeping you hidden and always afraid
Shame has a way to keep the door closed
Hiding yourself, nothing exposed

The lies of shame will keep you bound
Until one day the truth is found.
From which it came the origin is known
Til at last no more seeds to be sown

Breaking the lie that shame has told
Releasing you, from its very hold
Now to be all that the Creator has said
Not looking back, but only ahead

I pray that this book has encouraged its readers to continue and walk through the valley of ashes.

As the truth of Jesus Christ has set me free, I pray that you find freedom to achieve all the hopes and dreams that perhaps lie dormant amongst ashes.

If you are in prison and you read this book, I pray that God release you not only from prison bars, but from the prison inside your heart that led you there.

If you are in a rehabilitation center, I pray that God release you from the things that hold you bound.

I pray ashes to be turned to beauty on everyone who reads this book.

I pray you find the truth in Jesus Christ as I have and find a quiet place where you can begin to speak to him about the very secrets in your heart.

Bible Verse- Psalm 91:1 (New International Version)

"He who dwells in the shelter of the most High, will rest in the shadows of the Almighty. I will say of the Lord. "He is my refuge and my fortress, my God, in whom I will trust"

Peace Poem

Is it a place of solace and still
Is it sitting on a mountain or the highest hill
Is it the beach with cool waters rippling by
Is it the silence as we gaze into the clear blue sky

Peace is a state of mind, you find yourself in
A heart and soul that is gentle within
Calmness and joy encumbered around
Amid trouble this can be found

How it comes and how it goes
A mystery for some, for not everyone knows
Tis a secret for you surely to find
For this is the way for governing your mind

First to put trust in the one who does care
Making your burdens light and easy to bear
There's always a way through the weight of your load
As you are led by peace you will walk the right road

www.ingramcontent.com/pod-product-compliance
Lightning Source LLC
Chambersburg PA
CBHW052207070526
44585CB00017B/2100